SEX, DEATH & TRAVEL

For Patrick (FFriesen)
good to see you
enjoy + keep writing
Cheers
mona
CBA

Sex, Death & Travel

Prose Poems

by

Mona Fertig

OOLICHAN BOOKS

LANTZVILLE, BRITISH COLUMBIA, CANADA

1998

Canadian Cataloguing in Publication Data

>Fertig, Mona, 1954
>Sex, death and travel

Poems.
ISBN 0-88982-169-0

1. Prose poems, Canadian (English)* I. Title.
PS8561.E79S48 1998   C811'.54   C98-910285-8
PR9199.3.F47S48 1998

We acknowledge the support of the Canada Council for the Arts for our publishing programme.

THE CANADA COUNCIL | LE CONSEIL DES ARTS
FOR THE ARTS | DU CANADA
SINCE 1957 | DEPUIS 1957

Grateful acknowledgement is also made to the BC Ministry of Tourism, Small Businesss and Culture for their financial support.

We acknowledge the financial support of the Government of Canada through the Book Publishing Industry Development Program for our publishing activities.

Published by
Oolichan Books
P.O. Box 10, Lantzville
British Columbia, Canada
V0R 2H0

Printed in Canada by
Morriss Printing Company
Victoria, British Columbia

A trine of L O V E

Acknowledgements

Special thanks to *Cathy Ford, Maxine Gadd, Penn Kemp, Sandi Johnson, Annie Knoop, Kathy Venter* and *Phyllis Webb* for succour, friendship and feedback during the writing of these poems.

And to the people of Salt Spring Island who loved *Mango Woman*.

Thanks to Barb's Buns where the worksheets of these poems-in-progress were first displayed.

Some of these prose poems have appeared in:

Vintage '92, League of Canadian Poets Anthology (Sono Nis, 1992), A *Labour of Love* (Polestar Press, 1989), *Mango Woman* (Limited Edition Chapbook, (m)Öthêr Tøñgué Press, 1996), and *The Capilano Review*.

I sincerely thank The Canada Council and The British Columbia Arts Council for time and financial support in completing this manuscript which began in 1983. I also wish to thank the Banff Centre of Fine Arts, *especially Robert Kroetsch*, for being there.

Cover painting: oil on canvas by George Fertig. Untitled. 1982.

Author photograph by Derrick Lundy for *The Driftwood*. June 1996.

"Anything that comes upon you with this intensity you experience as numinous, no matter whether you call it divine or devilish or just 'fate'."

—C. G. Jung

Contents

Travel

Epilogue

Prologue

"When I write . . . I use the book like dynamite to blast myself out of isolation."

—Anaïs Ninn

Naming the Silence

In the warm kitchen she makes soup, watches over the death of herself. Steam covers the windows. Upstairs her writing room is a cube of cold. Deep in the brown ground, she feels the damp cloak of blindness, *the fur of the rat*, spidery roots; imagines diffused light across naked stones; hears underground water. Her potato head rests like a heart in the cellar, like a bone without sun, tossing and tossing in sheets of earth. A pearly blanket fresh with the delicate clues of winter birds covers her. *Shadows fall from a gothic moon.*

Sometimes she wakes up to the smell of Bad Poetry, broken pencils, a lead pain across her grey eyes. Her snowy self-rising. She blames other things, the nurturing breast, *the Perfectionist*. She repents, runs her hands through water, cleans the house, curses her Imagination. Hungers for visitors, summer fruit, a radiating joy along the base of her spine. Distant sounds of children lift and scatter like ravens, small angels, *demons*, exquisite hours in the scented afternoon. She sleeps, her eyes rolling back, tied and untied by the dream. But when she wakes she writes Nothing, captures Nothing. *Sweet Nothing at all.*

She bends to plant bulbs, pulls out old cornstalks for burning, makes apple pies, reads by the woodstove's warmth, the children long ago in bed. With her blood called ink, she scratches *turtle words* on an old face of paper. Her room overlooks the sea. She dreams her words become pinpoints of light, *extinct birds making a comeback*. She sets bountiful polished seed in the garden.

She warms her hands in the apricot sun, hears bells of laughter ringing, wings of birds invisible behind pines. She patiently works and reworks her poems, feels the swooping ache of perfect words, a thrumming and unexpected radiance. Her pen flowers, sunshine sweeps across the lilacs, the magnolia's monumental blooming. Everything surprises her. Her friends float by waving flags of tulips & daffodils. The taste of Victory fevers & embellishes her heart. She unexpectedly corners Silence, drowns in the River. *Time sweetens and sweetens her name.*

Sex

Mango Woman

On a hot tropical beach she slices ripe oval mangoes, *dripping* sweet orange fruit. Bends the peel back again and again into *tangerine* crescent moons. Sweet squares. Offers pieces to you. She is *suntanned, luscious;* a pandanus tree shades her eyes. You are *electric, summoned.* Have a desire for. Your hand around her wrist. *Waist.* The (brown ankles) turning in the sand. The salt (nut) scent of. She falling into you. The lush (body) taste of. Her watermelon nipples. *Almond areolas,* as smooth as butter cream. *Mangoes.* Nothing else touches your naked chest. Her throat curves towards the rumpus coral sea, a melon sunset. *Passionate mouths.* Saying (more and) no more. You dream of your separateness unbinding, losing shape. You drown in each other like torrential rain. Bodies feeling too much. You are as smooth & as firm as a porpoise. *Hot waists, a comet plunging through rings of Saturn.* Love leaves good marks in the soft white. *All night, sky* (as plush) (as quiet) as mango, peach, banana, papaya. *Couple as still life.* Asleep under the Southern Cross. Heat thunders like a dream.

Woman Who Runs With Wolves

She has left the tiny town. She is as wild as an eagle, clever and clear as a winter stream. She has left her husband, her friends, her children, the mortgaged house, the tame confining weight of books & fences. She has done this suddenly. Like a phone call from earth. She just threw up her hands and said, *I'm coming!*

This is the story she tells the wolves. They read her like a book. They are her friends, *her lovers*. Their fur, silver brown waves, deep black currents, her fingers *run/relish* through. They have found her & led her to a secret cave, dry & high in the misty forested mountains.

She teaches them not to be afraid of the fire she makes; it is the same fire that burns in their eyes. They bring her fresh sweet lamb, farm chicken. She plucks and skins, roasts the meat over hot alder flames. Their teeth do not frighten her.

After dinner they clean their fur, then lick her, from head to toe. Over the shells of her eyelids, down her neck, her pendulous smooth breasts, her erect nipples; their wet tongues slide down her arched back the slopes of her buttocks, over her supple belly, slowly between her open legs, *too tenderly.* Their heated wolf breath. Their warm wolf tongues. The scent of sex and wolf fur, *trembling bones.*

Once a month during the full moon they turn back into beautiful wild-hearted men. She chooses the best storyteller to make love to. *Satiated appetites.* This is a night that never ends. The rest of the men leave the cave for town dance halls, the loving beds of wild & free women.

She lives a long & enchanted life. Runs with the pack in spring, her willowy legs sensual as deer thighs. Her hair a long mane that smells of arbutus leaves on dry rock, sunlight on cedar boughs, smokey alder flames. *Legends surface like pink blossoms.* Flock like blue jays above the town.

The wolves would die for her. They believe she is the moon goddess. Such moon breasts, such moon belly, such moon eyes. They would sacrifice their last meal for her, go lean as pines in winter. Men in the village roll restlessly in their beds. Turn to their women when they hear the wolves. Make love with a slow hungry fever. Close their soft animal eyes.

Spring Fever or
You Can Have Your Cake & Eat It Too
(for all the married women)

Walking through town she unexpectedly turns into his hungry warm eyes, his seductive black wavy piano hair, his animus blue eyes; his hands float gentle as May magnolia.

She turns into the short driveway of his sentences, turns into the aroma of French roast coffee, *the low-down hip ache* of desire, the raspberry-chocolate lips of handsome men. Attraction burns through blue denim, under pale silk blouses, *bodies splashed by light.* She is luscious. Her smile offers him adventure. She kisses him once, wets him with her beauty. He tastes like a licorice devil, *undomesticated.* She rolls him around in her foxglove mouth, *devours him.* He leaves her unravelled. The world is dangerously fresh. Renewed. Radiant.

Feverish, she walks home uphill past thrusting red tulips, the small creamy nipples of snowdrops, pink tulips splayed open. Past the aroma of fresh baked bread, black forest cake. *Hands kneading.*

She comes home smiling and kisses her husband. Leads him to the bedroom. Undresses. Coaxes awake the honeyed fever of erections. Slow hands drive her crazy. She mounts her lusty dark-haired lover. They rock the skyblue sheets into bluer dust. Throaty sounds bring the mating birds to their window, even the panting cats and dog to their bed. *A warm shaft of sun inside apple firm thighs. The room covets passion.* The kiss, a delicious appetiser, blossoms mischievously, *unrepentant* overhead.

Men Kept Falling Into Her Eyes
Some Drowned There

All that summer, men kept falling unexpectedly into her eyes, into her lamp black irises, calm lake waters. She doesn't remember how it all began.

The first week, a handsome man drowned there. An afternoon treat. She told him to grab on to her dark combed eyebrows, grab onto their soft wings and she'd fly him free, but he wouldn't listen. He wanted to stay there *forever*, drowning above her radiant smile. Now he's gone, floating around somewhere in her mind like a log in a lake. She feels responsible, slightly guilty; his wife says he hasn't come home yet, the police are still searching for him. All she did was look *into* him and he disappeared.

Next, two fine men fell in; one came into the shop where she worked, and splash, that was it; he slipped on her tanned cheeks, saw something he wanted and dove right in looking for *treasure*. He was a good swimmer, so he escaped her deep undertow, climbed out exhausted but happy. *A golden coin like love warm in his palm.*

She invited the last one into her warm as a hot tub eyes. She was enjoying herself. So she let him swim in her sunny vacation lake where he floated on his back for awhile drinking margaritas, pretending he was in Mexico. He wouldn't leave and she realized she didn't want him to. She couldn't stop thinking about him, looking at him, into him. She wanted to swim out & offer him a meal, dessert. She became obsessed; *sex sex sex* was all she could think of.

Then he started to paddle towards the shade of her sunset lips, bronze arms stretching, dark eyes on fire. He began sucking on grapes, the sweetness of papaw, took a slow climb between her melon breasts. He kept travelling further, deeper. *His phallus amaryllis blooming. Enjoy* her body said. And she did. They both did. *Afterwards he came out wet and grinning.* Swam back up to her eyes. He was just warming up, she could tell and so was she, but she decided enough was enough. Pleasure was addictive and she had an addictive personality. So she walked away (*as cool as a summer popsicle*). Promised herself no more treats. She would buy sunglasses, avert her eyes, *stay home & work fertile miracles in her garden.* Look at trees, the failing shapes of flowers, wait for autumn mushrooms. Put up signs like *No Trespassing,* private lake, *mirror, woman.* Come back next summer.

Taboo Sex

They fucked for the passionate first time and the gentle last. They fucked on, a peaceful summer beach, in a brassy new city. They made love to the beautiful *genesis* of the world, and all its tragic decline.

The rumpled sunny bed, the faded living room sofa, the fragrant summer field melted away. The island could have buckled and tipped. They noticed nothing except Hunger & Thirst. The speed their clothes vanished. The aching atlas of their bodies. Lover's tongues. Closed eyes, clear backs. The man fitted the woman so *perfectly*. The *gorgeous* spacious sky of a woman. She squeezed/pulled him deeper. Up to her waist. He was a hard tawny arbutus. All night the *rocking* tight cave. Her circular breasts rose & fell, *inside coursed the salty sea.* Throbbing stars. Sleep. Then the Universe spiralling open once again. She took him into her like a finger into a mouth. *Sucked.*

They were noisy black cats, shy birds, wild sweaty horses, breezy butterflies, biting dogs, soundless snakes, silky white rabbits, quick mink, the thirsty, burning flesh of the desert. The passionate line, *landscape,* of the body, peeled back, sounding, letting go. They were the world desperately re-making itself. Joined so well, *so divinely*, they wanted to stay that way forever. Die that way.

They fucked for the foremost and tender last time. They fucked in a lush viridian forest, in a friendless winter city. They made love to the past & the future, the final couple left. *United.* They centred the dying earth, breathed life into each other's mouths. *Saved the world again and again.*

Traveller Beds Dream

She wants to sink deeper in to this horizon. *A sweep of violet reaching as far as the delirious eye can see, as deep as your hands will plunge. Jacarandas.* Sensuous blossoms. Joyous as a new body of love. She wants to stop this ebony train. This hot sleek machine snaking through New South Wales savannah. She wants to step off & be pulled down in this enchantment, in the middle of this private lush land. Heat of December. *Australia. She holds her breath.* Pink feathers, parrots, *gallairds* tremble in lavender branches. *Holds her breath again.* This is like love. This desire, this intoxication (this suffocation). She sweats like a butterfly in a jar, fertile, caught. *Explosions delayed.* Thighs ache. Come darkness she'll drown feverishly in her first fresh frangipani. Come easily in its soft golden centre. Creamy sides. Smooth as silk. *Sheets.* Landscape covers her, lips to petal, stamen. Woman beds dream.

Penis Flower

In the middle of our kitchen table your long electric
green stalk pumps forth mint stars, *drowsy bees.* Unfurls
butterscotch ardour. Spreads blushing fire south. Points
winter northward, gives it the boot. Washes Greek kitchen
rose doré, lilac pink, creamy white. Couples water. Outside
the frozen pavement is mystic blue with piled snow; ice
cuts us with its glass chill, five degrees below zero. Snow
measures up to our bundled waists. How far up do the
black fur-lined boots go? Inside, our amaryllis steams.
Warms the house. Pushes forth luxurious cinnamon blos-
soms in time to the fire crackling in the wood stove. Ban-
ners of petal-red scarves. Fat flowers the circumference of
silk pillows. You put your whole face in and sigh. *Scarlet
movies play. Brilliant tamarillos are bought. Juicy mangoes
devoured.* Red Cuban bananas peeled. You invoke mating
animals, *penis of bull, chocolate horses, naked oiled gods. Lusty
seamen.* Our cockatiels mate beside you in their cage. Out-
side winter watches. The male rocks on the grey back of
the female, small perky noises logging in his throat. Their
yellow crests high. Orange pancake cheeks blooming. You
long for the tight insides of women, *goddesses.* I hear you

sigh. You crave more pollinating bees. Their tiny stinging
kisses. You sigh again. Velvet tongues that polish pearls.
Mouth around your firm flesh, hands cupping *ripe figs*. A
winter romance. In the middle of January, your magic green
wand manifests the tropics, *the hothouse tango, orchids open-
ing at night,* sex as smooth as ice cream.

The Last Salmon Man

The woman drops her shiny balls of apples and crosses the October orchard. She sucks her waist in. Here comes the king of fish. She spies silver bodies hurdling underwater, toughened by money or politics. *Chinook.* Sterling sockeye. Electric blue spring. Then gentled again by daydreams of coitus. *Rain falling. Romance. Torn and tireless gods.* Battling up the fish ladder. Boiling under white water. *Close as socks.* Sharing cigarettes, stories. *Going homeward. Bornward.* Driven like storms. *Small children cradled pink in their souls.* Scales shimmer like ar/mour. The sweet music of fish sliding underwater. Smell of musky fins, moustaches, pewter beards, saltsweat hands of renovations, farms. *Mounds of seaweed, pints of beer and thick ink.* Tails that turn your head away from pruning and mending.

The woman smiles as she leans over the bank. Beckons the school with sly fingers, *firm pink hootchies.* A dinner of breasts. Entices a prince into her tepid bath of hands. His breath keelhauling under his heart. He gasps for love. Her paring knife traces his gills. *Her kisses leave him speechless.* Afterwards she ties back her river-washed hair. Zips up her bluejeans, *tough as stones. Scales glisten on the delicate insides of her thighs.* She sings like a seal across the banks of the old village. *Beware of that one, or, he rides like a stream.* Between her legs the rich spermscent lingers. *Invisible as krill.* She is reluctant to wash. Inhales life between rowing and casting her hook again.

Clouds blow by as the last salmon swims into a pothole. Grief burning his eyes like smoke. Mouth tasting of iodine & steel. The riverbed rocks him for days. With one eye towards shore his blood becomes a trail of pink ribbon in the sorry sorry light. *The woman cries.* Awards herself tears. *Her ovaries are luminous.* Nodding mooneggs bending in the autumn sky. She traces the rib of trees; *hard cold apples lie at her feet.* Evening mist softens a curve of squash. She leans over the cornsyrupy river. Her finger pokes through glass air. *Cold to the bone. Tiny parchment hearts peel off with time. Belated.* Love rises like mist off the lilypad of her tongue.

Death

To Our Child Sleeping
With Sorrow
I Have Not Forgotten You

There is a magic bean growing inside of me. Floating next to a grief that is veiled and weary. There is a star sparkling in the darkness, in the cave of all beginnings, and I speak to you and say, do not fear what is inside of me. This mourning is made of love and love; it cries during its season, then sinks back into the heaving cycles of sun and sleeping. It is Sorrow but do not be afraid to reach out and touch it. It will not harm or curse or bear malice or anger. *This grief is not a cold stranger.* It is a swollen heart, a hundred days of solitude, the whole rainy universe going on forever. It is autumn brittle with loss. Burnt umber paper hearts crackle as they drift past your tiny alabaster face. Your illuminated body dreams on. For awhile you will be a companion to Sorrow. Sleep and wake next to its tired body. Grief's face worn thin from looking backward, gone into the saddest dream. But one day you will be alone and shining, larger than your watery world. The small rays of your pink petaled face finally pushing forth and again. Pushing forth and again. Into a warm and paramount room.

Abduction

I'm three and a man walks up to me and asks me to get into his truck. I'm three and I'm cranky and I'm at my new play school and it's sunny and warm. My sister who's seven, yells "NO!" from our car and the man leaves. *Leaves me alone.* I don't know why he talked to me. His shirt is bright red like my pajamas. Like balloons. I'm tired. I'm three and I'm a big boy. I heard my sister yell "NO!" My mom is getting my things.

August passes. The RCMP investigate. My husband returns from out-of-town. He wants to find and kill this stranger. I hear other island stories about that devil-red truck. My son's narrow escape puts me on Red Alert. Time only deepens my fear. Takes me to an Ancient place. To the cave of a thousand years of bonding. In a dark corner lies the Nightmare Box. The lid is blasted off. My son's face postered "Missing" on every shop window. His nightmare crying tortures me. Splits my soul. My arms circle and circle him. Forever.

The danger of men gone sour. Invisible dangers. Those soft folds of fathers, brothers, uncles and grandfathers. A trusted friend a warm smile a neighbour's lap. Now who can you trust? Whose child will be approached next? An innocent valentine red shirt. *Hanging. That fiery truck.* The shadows that dance with long adult fingers pulling at children's joyous feet. Pulling them down into the longest darkest shadow of their life. *Fifteen minutes missing at the Fall Fair.* A disguised Snakeman with his molesting oyster hands slithers his way unobtrusively behind jars of homemade jams. Fresh and brilliant cardinal flowers. *A slaughtered lamb's thigh.* Barrels and barrels of orchard red apples. Squeezed to the drinking point.

His forked tongue offers heart candy and my little boy says, "Yes." My eyes and heels dizzily click and spin. Like a Mother-of-the-World I nervously pivot for danger. There are thieves that will steal your child-gold from under your thumb. We must cut off their hands. Use X-ray eyes on their hearts. We must protect our children. *Claim them. Warn them. Arm them.* With our lives.

I say to you. To the stranger who dared in his shouting red shirt and his red as a poison-apple truck. *Red is my son's blood.* Red as a mother's revenge. You in your arrogance. You with your hands full of casual death. Waiting outside daycares. You who could live here. Could be sitting in this audience. You whom somebody knows by name, befriends. *Beware.* We will corner you. Make you visible. Circle you with fire and hate. Put gloves on and pull you in like a fat and stunned rat. *Annihil/hate you.* Publicly. Bring back the cat-o'-nine-tails. The public hanging. *The eye for an eye.* For I have a mother's true sight now. Deep instinct, to cushion the fear. I can envision history and the future all at once. One long waiting room full of tormented grieving mothers who will *honestly* do terrible things with sharp knives that go *click* when you sleep. So you will never sleep peacefully. *Never sleep peacefully again.*

I Feel Like Sisyphus

I help my mother to another rest stop. Her body slow with disbelief. Her sorrow *unnameable*. I close my pounding salteyes. *O noon sun spare me.* For comfort I dream of my childhood home on Pioneer Ave. It rises happily. A large wooden house I anchor to. There I'm a quiet teenager. My dad is downstairs, *alive and painting.* Spring sun melts through my bedroom window, spreads golden across my desk, my floor. But a mirage shudders on the horizon, and my father dies and reappears again and again. My mother is drowning. Grief cements her ankles. Her heart flutters in a coma. I hold on to her widowed hands. I call out a safety line, but all she hears is my father's voice evaporating like mist. *She goes under for the third time.*

I am the daughter. *I am the other mourning one.* I feel like Sisyphus carrying the stones of sorrow, and the sky is ocean and tomorrow is another mountain. I feel like shouting No air, No air, No more! O mother I want to sleep forever. I am exhausted. Bring me comfort and flowers. *Bring me your mothering.* My limp hair roots weakly into my cotton pillow. Searching for a life line. Only the passage of time relieves me. Slowly, I am saved from drowning. *My mouth empties and empties its despair.*

"This death is no external enemy, it is his own inner longing for the stillness and profound peace of the all-knowing non-existence, for all-seeing sleep in the ocean of coming-to-be and passing away."

—Carl G. Jung

Father, Father

There is that phone call of Death, and a deep sobbing, sobbing. There is pure shock and the body ringing. There is this terrible pit, this house of angry grief where I struggle like a hostage, a non-believer, *a blinded eye.* To keep clear. Open like an antenna for your messages, your guidance. *Your miraculous return.* But inside my lifelines pump and flow in dumb circles. The sky has exploded and I cut myself again and again on your name. *Invisibly I bleed. Alone.* On street corners. With friends. Often before saviour sleep. *An ocean of sound held back held back.* Now I can only imagine your face, and it says never again will I see you. Now I can only imagine your voice, and it says never again will I hear you. I've taken the years of sad dreams and placed them in a book. Why couldn't they prepare or protect our hearts, the soft underbellies of love, for the blows that would come? In one dream you lay dying and said to me, *"Accept it."* I long to turn back time. Pronounce all memories the best. After the funeral, as the white hearse drove away, after the graveside visit, beneath the willow by the tiny brook. I wanted to believe you didn't lie static below but stood luminous beside us. A part of something more than we could ever imagine. Your arms around our shoulders, the background fading. Not because of the tears, but because of the soft inaccessible place you have taken us to. Do not leave us there. *Perform miracles*. Death has elevated you. But we have become faces heavy as beggars. *Kneeling for our lives.*

Beliefs Waiting For The World

In the mirror and out, slips truth, foreboding, exalting. The twinning paradoxes of Life and Death. Your ghost stands behind me. *So eloquent and frayed.* Nearly the fog of your breath on glass. Nearly your presence. My search for answers begins. In your books, your <u>underlined</u> passages surround me as I read deeper into my life.

Sitting under the blossoming cherry tree in our backyard, the quiet forget-me-not flames of your eyes ignite as sky. Those same eyes that in my childhood could turn and turn me to stone. I remember the sound of your brush against *canvas, linen, burlap, silk.* Your happiness when you were left undisturbed. *Your eyes as soft as watercolours.*

For years your paintings sanctified our living room. Outlined the perimeters of two sisters blooming shyly around the kitchen table. In our bedrooms we imitated your solitude. Were not social butterflies. Felt the invisible presence of Moons, Alchemist's bowls, Fruit and Oceans, that glowed like deities below. Upstairs we daydreamed. Clusters of honey and licorice butterflies sailed like friends into our rooms.

Your need to create, to paint, was synonymous with life. Year after year you struggled. Aging. Unknown. Each breath a little harder. A caustic wit gathering greyly at your brow. Can I learn strength from your failures? Your perseverance? Can I face my poetry alone in the night? Birthing year after year into a empty room?

Artist. Teacher. Philosopher. You were father father. Failing and excelling. Your quiet obsession. Your oily canvases breaking and breaking like illuminated waves against the frontier coast. Against the blind custodians of art. Your paintings with their open moon arms comforted you. Pulled you in and tempered your separation, *your exile*, with a soft otherworld glow.

The March wind and another year passes. The snowdrops crown your unmarked grave. Your bones lie as fragile as gold leaf. Returning to the Great Mother. A delicate tree, a willow, unfurls its green ribbons above you. And over the hill in my mother's dark closet, your paintings sit. Like holy disciples. *Patient and shining.* Children of the unconscious. *Beliefs waiting for the world.*

The Suitcase

It's taken over fourteen years to write this poem. About the suitcase of your burial clothes I carried to the funeral parlour. The long walk past the insipid plastic flowers towards the blacksuited saleswoman of Death. In the next room waited the ornate sarcophaguses, *frilled satin beds,* the wine-flushed expensive coffins. We chose the simplest. The cheapest. (As if money were the question.) Even asked if we could build our own.

I lifted the brown suitcase across the counter so the mortician could redress you. Yank grey wool socks onto your cold feet, *no shoes.* (*Where you were going you would be flying.*) Drag on old trousers, push your thin white arms into your favourite shirt, the beige corduroy jacket you liked. (*As if this would comfort you, keep you warm.*) My mother had put coins in your pocket for good-luck, *for the journey across the dark starless river.* Your favourite book by Carl Jung to accompany your mind, our wedding photograph (*taken only two months earlier, the day you said you were so happy*). My best poem to burn its singing fragility into your soul.

When the woman at the counter asked if I wanted to see you, *one last time,* I said "No!" My voice sad against the ugly walls. (*I wanted to remember you alive, sitting at our home two weeks earlier in the lazy September sun, eating your favourite lunch; a beer and a cheese sandwich. Sadness and wit, twins circling your eyes.*) The woman disappeared but quickly returned, handing me back your old suitcase, a leather shell, *a bomb from the Death Room.*

My heart imploded. I held on, *reeling fast.* In my hands hung crumpled clothes. Seamed pants, an undershirt and suspenders that had once outlined your body, but had failed to support you, *heart stopping,* as you fell to the floor. *My mother holding you. ("Forgive me," the last words from your pale lips.)* In the corner stood your easel, cleaned just days before, your brushes dried and put away. The last canvas finished. *In nightmares you are never in control. You must follow the heavy choking black thread to the end or wake screaming.*

Like a Perennial
(for Marguerite Pinney)

The twilight sky is soft with watercolour violets.
Evening-scented stock. *Nicotiana.* I contemplate the Death
that has come to claim you. A third time. A persistent
octopus whose inky clouds fill your face with pain. I visit
you beneath the emerald mountains. I give you a ruby dress
to wear. You look so brown & healthy. (*I dream you are
only pretending to die; that you disappear happily out the door
with a companion to start a new life.*) I think of you under
the cool fragrant mountains on Pasley Island in this ripe
coastal summer. I think of how your geraniums are defi-
antly strawberry red. The lemon roses heavenly. You plant
scarlet runner beans and race them to the finish. Life vi-
brates through these perennials. In the centre of such fi-
nality you bravely pour tea. Believe in reincarnation. Bed
with thorns of pain. (*The garden can be possessive of its love.*)
You say you are not afraid to die. Your courage impassions
me. My problems shrink to the size of worry beads. Child's
marbles. *Temporal and ordinary.* For many evenings I think
of the shape of fate. The shadows and light that form and
follow each person. How your daughter was thrown from

a horse. Thrown into another world. Her exuberant life hospitalised. *You holding and holding your baby again.* Feeling your whole heart break—is this where the end began? Mourning glories in your hair. Death finding a window in. In autumn an ardent fire consumes you. You as ashes. You as dust. *Each spring, you I will remember.*

Letters To My Mother

Dear mother,
you feel wronged, mother-in-law to the wrong man. Dis-
taste rings your mouth, does not beg for forgiveness. *Spit
flies through the phone.*

Dear mother,
let's get down to facts; *emotional abuse* is against the law,
nineteen years is long enough. I hate *your Scorpio lovebite.*

Dear mother,
I ride the rollercoaster of daughterhood. You make me sick.
You make me happy. I call for the doctor. I pray for your
warm motherly love, *smooth hands, arms as plush as velvet.*

Dear mother,
you see me as the stolen daughter married to a clever thief.
I see you as *the mother I promise never to become.*

Dear mother,
you have cancer; they held the knife to your breast and
your daughters came running. All summer we cared for
you; our home was your healing place. Slowly you moved
upstairs, felt better; *loneliness brought forth your best mask.*

Dear mother,
you throw the Ace of Spades, fortune or fate. You shuffle
your cards again and again. *O if I could heal you with a kiss.*

Dear mother,
the wounded daughter seeks relief. Wants to say No, no
more to her mother, wants to fear her less. Wants to love
her simply, to the lip of her grave. But your words are thin-
ner than needles, carefully placed, *your craft beads a tor-
tured history.*

Dear mother,
I love you, but the pain you've given me bites like a whip.
You keep trying to strike me, hook my love, my attention.
You keep trying to undermine *this house of love.*

Dear mother,
our life is fulfilling, private, *resplendent;* you are dangerous
inside it. *How much more can my heart take?*

I Opened My Clamshell Mouth
And Howled

My mother's apartment shook as my sister told me, *"Nothing's for you, everything's to go to me."* Our mother lay dying in St. Paul's hospital on the hill above all this and this. *No Will. The crown of thorns swayed in its pot. Vermilion blossoms trembled and dripped like blood.* Stabbed in the back, I opened my clamshell mouth and howled. *Through a watery curtain,* I saw meanness so startling. So frightening. Insensitivity, a dark circle around my sister's dumb mouth.

For days the heavens outside rained *broken glass, bullet sand, razor clams.* "Mom wanted to hurt you after she died." More words like lightning tore through my soul, *burned my eyes out,* shot deep underground, *ripped apart the small family roots, the sensitive hearts of trees.* Lawns broke open. *Frantic fissures.* The small sleeping shells of wasps flew forth. Kind maples bowed and caught my crying in their arms. Tried to hold on to me. The sea looped around my white face, my flying hair. The September wind rocked me, sat me down on the old grey rocks. Blood poured from my back & stained the ocean, the sand a sticky blueblack. Paralysed, I fell into a bottomless grieving sleep.

When I awoke, I saw first the jagged limbs of broken trees, remembered the violent storm, a clamshell mouth howling. (*Was it my own?*) Stared at the horizon. Tried to hold on to something kind, *kind*. One memory. A *small boat*. But there was nothing. My mother forever silent, *underground. No Will*. My father turning in his grave. *No sister.*

All winter I saw the world as it really was, and vomited pain. All winter the shock of betrayal reeled like a tornado around me. I called my sister *liar, bitch, betrayer*. Stopped the bleeding. Applied pressure. Disconnected the phone. Will never forget those who helped me. Forgo. But I can not forgive. *A sister is not as precious as an eye. The blade in the heart has left a wound deep as a canyon.*

Funeral Song

Giving birth to my daughter, two days of hard labour, was the most agonising work my body ever had to do. Watching my mother die for three days was the most agonising work my soul ever had to do.

I stroked her short grey hair, placed my thumb gently at the centre of her forehead. This is where the door of *blameless light* will open. This is where storms of polar fear will exit. *Sad sleeper.* Melt down the slope of your smooth face. *Soft olive skin.* Float *like ghost birds* down the hospital corridor. Blow away as moon dust. *Evaporate one lie at a time.* My mother's mute sleep a spanning dungeon. An ultimate metamorphosis. *A webbing orange breast cancer smothering her brain.*

Once you lifted your long arms & said, *"I'm coming,"* and *"I see her."* Who did you see? I held dried lavender to your nostrils; they quivered. You wrinkled your eyebrows still black as the glossy wings of ravens. *I remember you so gypsy-beautiful.* And with a last amazing effort you turned your paralysed body and said my name. . . . We will meet again when I die, I told you; you will be there to gather me in. One clear tear answered. When I lifted an eyelid so you could see me, *eldest daughter*, I saw your pupils, milky, blind as marbles.

On the last night I sat till twilight by the large hospital window listening to your moist breath. *Your death rattle.* The north shore mountains, the city you loved, the evening tide, so vibrant against my grieving back. I wanted to get into your narrow bed and hold you, but instead I ran my fingers slowly across the strings of a small handmade lyre. I played as the sky turned a spreading cobalt violet, *a mourning shawl around me.* A handful of stars started to shine. *This is my good-bye song.* I whispered, "*I love you.*" My voice diamonded by tears. (*Hearing is the last sense to go.*) The city sparkled through that awful awful night.

A few days later, home on Salt Spring Island, I dreamed you lay down on my son's bed. *You were tired and said you'd been on a long journey, and could only visit for a short while.* There was *such Life, such Light* shining in your eyes.

Inheritance

My mother gave me her large houseboat of aluminium
I always bake my turkey in, the secret sage and apple stuff-
ing I love. How to make Bavarian apple pie, a little butter
on top before you seal the crust, a milk wash brushed over
the scent of fresh apples, hot & baking. My mother gave
bread and butter to the kids when they were hungry. *Sim-
ply put. It satisfies.*

She taught her granddaughter, Sophia, how to draw
faces when she was three & four, coloured crayon lines
around a plate, enough space for a smile and bright crooked
eyes. These drawings she kept for months hung on her
fridge. I found them saved in her drawer after she died.
She used to let Sophia play crazy cook, mix flour, salt, sugar,
raisins & herbs all in one wild mess. All over the kitchen
counter & on the floor. She loved to read to her and take
her to the beach. She gave her grandson, Paris, a magnify-
ing glass, a fragile amber glass owl when he was three; she
knew he was old enough to treat it special, especially from
granny. She knew he would love music by the shape of his
ears, saw the rhythm in his eyes, his bouncing fingers. She
gave him coins & purses for the money he would have.

My mother showed me how to comb my dark eyebrows, *lucky the women who inherit them.* Strength from a clear brow. My mom showed me how to look after my health, but never went to a doctor herself until it was too late. Her beautiful slender hands gave me a necklace, many earrings, a pale see-through green Mexican dress I have yet to wear. My mother went with the kids and me on a wonderful evening walk along Kitsilano beach a year before she died. Took us for dinner on the corner of York St. near our old apartment. My favourite beach flourished with driftwood, *the sweet shells of childhood.*

After my mother died I coveted her sparkling amethyst beads, her old navy sweater, her grey rubber boots, her watch, *stopped.* Photographs. I wanted more. Her books, her memories. The handmade chicken teacosy pinned with hearts. Outside my window a woman walks up the hill. She reminds me of my mother. The stride of her legs. How my mother loved baseball, skating, cats, carrots, hated purple vegetables, how she always looked good. Dressed well. Was beautiful. How she was my father's muse. Gave her life for Art. Buried all her dreams, but one.

My mother gave me independence, a silver ring, the memory of a long-legged girl on Spanish Banks. She gave me her blood, her stories, her intuition. Palms held, teacups turned, tarot cards read and remembered. Passed on. Her mannerisms, sometimes the way I talk. I catch myself and hear her speaking. The shape of her laughter flying skyward. The shape of her hands. Her face.

My mother gave me her green thumb, her strong European body, her youthful olive skin, half of her beauty, the penny at the end of her nose. My mother gave me tenacity, gullibility, her love of music & dancing. Her love of solitude. Her love of people. *Her love.* My mother gave me life.

Travel

Christmas In Australia

On Christmas morning, long after the young wallaby has sat in the garden at 5:00 a.m., the kookaburra's sweeping laughter fills the small valley, heralds the heat. Here, on thirty-nine acres of lychees, mandarins, nectarines and bananas, the butcher bird parts the palms and hangs its prey. The peach trees *hum* with sleigh bells, wasps, a mysterious dreamy presence.

Inside, a feathery Australian conifer slimly waits, pink and green lights blinking slowly, in a bucket of sand. Sunshine pours through the windows. We open presents with new-found relatives; our children grin like Cheshire cats. By 9:00 a.m. the ghost gums *shimmer* in wings of heat. We drive past the Lebanese tourists to the beach, push our sandaled feet beyond the sleepy eyelids of long goannas, the lifting white wings of pelicans.

Into the burning sand we stick our beach umbrella, butter our skin with sunscreen, swim between the lifeguard's safety flags. Even on Christmas Day, below the surface are dangerous undertows, silent shapes of snow-white sharks, burning bluebottles. A frilled-neck dragon lizard scurries behind a sand dune. Floating overhead, in invisible summer dresses, a *choir of angels glimmer.*

I drag my toes in the smooth biscuit sand. Search the empty horizon. Drink in its boundless clarity. Down the beach teenage nephews balance on surfboards while we amateurs learn to bodysurf on rounds of waves. Our mermaid daughter goes underneath, holds hands with her aunt, becomes an expert in original warmth. Lightblue jelly fish as large as cats float by, *small stinging planets.* My daughter laughs and swings aside her long seaweed-black hair.

Down the beach the men happily dig for pippies, toes twisting deep into the sand. Hip-high in waves they cast out. Silver Bream in the green ocean lunge for soft clam meat, hook their lips on misunderstanding. I hold hands with my five-year-old son, walk between ocean and shore over red & purple volcanic rocks, through tidepools, soft bracelets of water around our ankles; a summer disc haloes our heads.

Later in the afternoon we play cricket under the shade of the eucalyptus trees, the old and the young, the click of the striped ball—Granny, Jim, the parents and the children, the crack of the whip bird. With binoculars I watch the yellow-tailed black cockatoos tip branches. *Pink bottle brush,* yellow jasmine, creamy frangipani bloom cool and languid. The dog sleeps under the mulberry bush, his tongue *panting.* We close our eyes, smell roasting turkey in the oven. There is no twilight *downunder.*

Mistletoe, cicadas, *holy night*, the rainbow lorikeets feed on bananas, a tree frog croaks on the tin roof. Down the hill a papaya hangs like an orange moon, tempts the hungry beaks of parrots. Wet black seeds *glisten* in the night. We have turkey dinner and homemade Christmas pudding with whipped cream and custard. *Jingle bells. Noel.* Between sherry, wine, along the long skin of the hours, a few old and precious stories.

Some Aussies longingly dream of a snowy Christmas. A time absent from this smokey humidity, the salty weight of perspiration. A day that is clear, cold, *mountainous as history*, an orange fire crackling on a hearth, a blue-eyed wind howling. *Icicles the length of kangaroo tails*. But I will always covet our hot Australian Christmas. *Long* to wear loose petal dresses again. Submerge, *submit* my body to the warm sea. The country that pressed itself, *a red dusty earth, a delicate sun orchid, an ancient platypus land*, into my skin, the long salty coastal line of my memory. Where I unknowingly felt the weight of Dreamtime, called it heat or Australia, did not recognise *mystery*.

Redback Spiders
& Goannas

After breakfast, toast and tea, we get ready for the beach. Slap on sunscreen, straw hats, cool sunglasses, big towels. My nine-year-old daughter slides open the glass door to get her runners. Slides outside. Ghost gums hum with early heat. Suddenly she shouts, "There's a redback spider in my shoe!" The day cracks open. Aunt Leonie leaps outside to knock the redback out of Sophia's runner before it can bite her. Expertly squashes it dead with a stick.

I am flooded with relief. The hospital is twenty long minutes away. Small bodies fill faster with poison. Identify your enemy. Specific anti-venom needs to be applied. Tiger Snake will attack if alarmed. One killed Uncle Fred's dog on this farm. Length 1.8 m. Highly toxic. Dial 000. *Keep calm*, wrap the bitten limb tightly. *Death could come in minutes.*

In this foreign landscape the tails of goannas can break the leg of a dog or a man. My daughter wants to take the redback home. A trophy. Like a lion-hunter. She has escaped gangrene, unknown agony. Earned a small black and red spider in a bottle. A resin-dipped sparkling pin for her bravery. But I say No. *A mother needs no reminders.*

Back home, at school, she recounts her story with elaborate gestures. Spreads more dangerous and exciting tales about Australia. True to nature we believe every one of them. Wombat grows to monstrous heights, *taipan snake, funnel-web spider* kills tourist, *saltie, crocodile,* swallows local. Box jellyfish, *sea wasp,* sends woman from sea screaming. She collapses on the beach, stops breathing. *Do not remove tentacles from skin.* Douse with vinegar. Call an ambulance. *Dial 000.*

Four Brothers

It's stifling hot. We're on the road again after a month on the sleepy fruit farm in Grassy Head, Australia. In the rear view mirror the one-story bungalow on the hill disappears, sun-tanned hands wave like palm fronds from the carport, the black bull, *Satan*, shrinks out of sight like a purple plum down a hall of grass.

Between family, *brothers*. The long blood tie. You can feel it stretching thinly between banana trees, past lilac jacarandas. It snaps like a whipbird, floats soft as farm dust over our skin. Tumbles over the netted peaches, hard buds of lychees, follows us like a fine spider thread the rest of our trip.

Forty years ago, four small boys. Childhood a state of stone and slate, old Liverpool streets, the call of the rag man, playing in bombed houses. The bathtub hanging on the outside wall, the fish and chip pan above the stove, jam butties, the poverty, *the outhouse cold as a bicycle.* No hot water. Bathnights, mom got in first, in front of the coal fire, the youngest (my husband) last.

Four mischievous boys in one bed laughing and fighting. Blood as thick as Marmite. *"Dead grotty, it's the gear."* Inside the windows, ice as thick as dinner plates. All winter sleeping in layers of clothes. Shining shoes on Saturday. Short pants. The canings at school, purple & yellow bruises the size of cigars, the length of rulers. Broken glass set in the backyard wall. Four small rooms, the teapot always full, layers of loose soft tea leaves, the dampness you could wring your hands around, dirty smog, stones through Catholic school windows, *never fish & chips on Fridays.*

Their mom & dad hard-working. The way things were, discipline & religion. Birthdays fell as quiet as pennies. Cats were swung against a wall. Anger. Love. *Visions on stairways.* A thin & strict Pentecostal God. *The world was created in six days. Woman was born from the rib of man.* Stealing through narrow treeless streets at night. Into trouble. Boys unfamiliar with the shapes of trees. Forests. Coats rich with the smell of the sea.

The youngest who drew & painted, who in secret made his own forbidden guitar and hid it under the bed. The brother who taught him to fight. How he ran away to Wales. Worried his mother, went fishing for dreams. Preached on street corners, *gave half his youth to the poor.*

These brothers, who left their mother country, for adulthood, for Australia. Two flew before, the family followed, through a hurricane off the coast of Spain, through the Suez Canal, just before the six-day war. They sailed into Australian heat, a sun that sucked the damp out of their

English bones, cured their mother's migraines, emptied their father's lungs. Turned them into Aussies, Kiwis, *whinging poms,* with wives, meat pies, barbies; new countrymen under sweltering skies.

We give one last wave from the jeep. The stiff gum trees swallow up the farm, the dusty road bends with sadness, leads us past emus, bower birds. Half way around the world.

Back home in Canada sits a snapshot of those young Liverpudlians. Happy, caught by the camera in an old black-and-white photograph. Sitting on a sandstone windowsill in their backyard with their father, *so long ago.* The world their apple, *whole, delicious, indivisible.*

Waiting for the Rainbow Lorikeets

We wait in the sweltering Gold Coast noon, *Surfers Paradise*, under Australia's brilliant skyeye. In a large circle we hold small tins, pewter-coloured pans full of sweet bread in sticky syrup. *Offerings.* Marking time. *Tender & still tourists.* Our throats dry with hope. Do not pause for *lolly water, icy-pole.* We are fair dills. Straw hats tipped backwards. Plastic sunglasses. Creamy sunscreen lotion. Our son, overheated, sunbaked, whinges, *wants to bail out,* see the black carpet snake, shady and dark. Lean against cool glass the length of the reptile king's body. But fenced dingoes, *caged boomers,* shy brown tree kangaroos wait with us. Look upward. Stretch their rubbery necks. It's so hot. Just a little bit longer. We scan the muggy sky past the silent blackbutt eucalyptus, the tray-wide sap-green leaves of strange trees. *Soon.* More than an hour crawls by. (*But I could wait forever.*)

Suddenly a waterfall noise of colour arcs the sky, surprises us, then rainbow wings disappear inside sheltering trees. We hold our offerings, our tired hands even higher. *For the birdgods.* Boomerang, the flock flies swiftly into the sky again. A cloud of lime wings, *hungry cherry beaks,* smokey silk-blue heads, new yellow chests, all trembling for sweet syrup, juicy nectar. They've been coming here for years. Sweat trickles down my arm. Dropping on burning cement. Steaming upward. It's 36°C. Red beaks dip voraciously into silver pans, *precious discs*. In the Land of Oz my prayers are answered. One rainbow lorikeet lands nervously on my head & another on my arm. I dream in Technicolor. I am touched by the featherweight of untamed beauty. I am still as a ghost gum. Smiling. Triumphant. *Rapturing in Currumbin.*

Travelling Past Bush Fires, Cyclone, Earthquake

Newspaper headlines: BLACK FRIDAY. 90 FIRES RAGE OUT OF CONTROL. 400,000 HECTARES ABLAZE! Photos of cuddly koalas, walnut-eyes burning, roasting at the top of gum groves, smoke curling from singed fur. A fierce crackling hurts the weekend air. Sugar gliders cook to death. Tree kangaroos impaled by the hot hard teeth of fire. *The inferno soil squeals.*

With a day's head start we motor muscle away. *Laane-corre.* On the left side of the road, in the white chocolate sun we spin halos, a muggy escape. *Dandaraga.* Melt through Yamba where a hundred Australian bikies, in black shiny lizard hides, fly by. *A lace monitor, a blue-tongued skink.* Their bodies spread atop chrome hogs, looking fierce. Middle-aged tongues darting. The goanna tail of the pack cuts the highway in half, incites accidents. *Hells Angels from Perth.* In an East Indian roadside cafe, my five-year-old son stares at their body of chains. I whisper, *don't look them in the eye.* We sit by a window in the dirty little booth eating samosas, drinking mango juice. Salty fries delicious on our tongues. The smell of smoke and Harleys confuse the air.

In Byron Bay, we bump into our eager surfie nephews. Bronze-skinned they soar by, bubble with coffee. Are sucked towards a cyclone blowing off the Gold Coast. Waxed boards strapped to their cars they lift off, mouths open, *blond hair flapping like wings.* In a trail of sunscreen, they disappear toward the biggest wave of their dreams.

Eleven towns we pass or eleven hours we drive, I can't remember which. January 5th. A choice of sleeping in a laundry room for $200 a night. *No rooms to let.* Nowhere to go but into the black caffeine night. This is the busiest tourist season of the year. I feel like old Mary. *Hail highways. Tea on the go.* The mind goes limp and puddly, the kids fall asleep, saggy dolls in the back seat. Hot wind pushing our car forward into the starry hills. We end up in Pottsville. *Motel wasteland,* tiny geckoes on a brick bedroom wall, the welcoming arms of two ugly beds. *Wind like hell ripping curtains of sand off the beach.*

We've been journeying north all day in the redback heat, *grong grong,* driving all day along the coast, *urunga.* Our ice-cream rental car, *air-conditioned refuge machine,* glides past burnt sugar cane fields, melting little towns, *derribong.* Sticky Queensland, licorice tar glues our tires to the road. I peel up my banana dress, spray water under my arms, sweaty thighs, mist our children in the back seat. They drink bright 7-Up, savoury chilled root beer, tangy cold lemonade, *waidup.* Between them a styrofoam cooler large as a white dingy, *thermoplastic ice cube,* crowds the car. Turns good little travellers into hotheaded prisoners. Crowded searing eyes. *Swiping mean.*

The Brisbane motel is no comfort in 44°C. One geriatric fan pushes muggy air in slow circles, cuts heat like a dull door cuts cheese. We drop useless clothes in the corner. Move like sloths. Exit from patio doors towards crystal blue pool-water, air-conditioned movie houses. *Thunder bullets the air.*

Escaping Australia we fly to Fiji in a rusty tin plane held together with duct tape. A crack in the seams. Dripping water. Turbulence shakes this toy. Thin metal separates sky from feet. The plane sharply ascends. We cannot land. Violent rain warns of a coming storm. We vibrate like trapped insects in a jar. *Our eyes rattle like stones. Die to fly free.* I watch our calm children for animal clues. There is no panic in their voices. In their calm eyes. But we remain nervous parents, *tightly buckled, so green.*

The cyclone finally hits Brisbane, ripping up varnished giant eucalyptus, blowing baked frogs up to the moon. On our tiny tropical island miles from Fiji we lie in our quiet buré. The sea is calm. Here we hope we are safe. If a storm comes I will bury down deep in the dusty ochre sand, move in with the large land crabs. Dig a cave till help comes. Protect my children with my *mother-till-I-die* body.

On Malolo Lailai, we postcard home, *All's well, having a great time.* Flying home to Canada we land unexpectedly in Hawaii where black 4" morning headlines, scream: EARTHQUAKE IN LA! Large photos of freeways and buildings buckled and burning. *Warzone.* Stop. *Looting.* Stop. *People traumatised.* Stop. Scorching ground fires. *Don't panic.* Stop. *Knackered,* in a cocoon of exhaustion, wearing sleeper's masks, we leave the tremulous world. Fly far up like anxious birds, *bimbimbie.* Home.

Malolo Lailai

36°C. After a hot three-hour ferry ride, we drift towards shore. Luggage thrown carelessly into a small *waiting, rocking* rowboat. *Teal sea, robin's-egg blue ocean, coral reefs teasing the hull.* Humidity smothers our bodies gathers above our hips, runs down our backs, *round waists, rivers of salt.* We unpack, hurry like dry sponges into the triumphant sucking sea. *Our wet bodies, soaked and slippery with shiny sun.*

In our buré we lift off flowered sulas, wet bathing suits. Shower often in the old ivory tiled bathroom, stand naked, *one body after another,* luke-warm saltwater running down our tanned healthy skins. *Hallelujah wafers,* small cakes of soap slippery in our hands. The noisy fan slices through heat thick and soft as butter. Over *melting moist bodies* its cool breeze leaves us spread-eagled. Outside a burning bush of white hibiscus, *languid silhouettes, a week of scented apparitions.* Coal-black mynahs perch in enormous mango trees. Tiny globes of shiny avocado-green fruit fall on dry pathways between rows of palms, their crisscrossed bark, *the direction our feet move.*

Bodies as flexible as plasticine, our heads hang limp, *our eyes open like lizards*. We sprawl on chairs, float timeless on water, quench our thirst, hover briefly under the medallion sun. "Bula," smile the Fijians. Black curly hair, bodies long, moving the way a quiet breeze moves through palms. In the kingbed as large as a raft we wonder at travelling so far across so much ocean. The night sky hot and dusty fingers the moon. A soft pearl. Pulls it closer. The children sleep, eyelids busy with tropical dreams. Thin pink sheets crumpled across honeyed skin. *Piles of wet towels, pyramids on the amber tiled floor.*

In the middle of the night something splashes in the toilet. I imagine flying fish, tailless geckoes, crabs with baked potato bodies rising up for their nightly crawl. They tunnel past dried rivers of sweat, brown earth, *limp pistils & stamens*. Their clicking claws move sideways outside toward tasty leathery lizards, *the planets of coconuts, dark & tender feet*.

I half listen to drums in the distance. Outside the falling thud of a hairy green coconut. The quick cut of a machete, a man's arms brown and shiny as burnt toffee, the taste of fresh clear milk, the coconut a chewy delicious white. The drums, the crab clicking go on all night, a code undeciphered, fading between love and sleep, between the cooling stars and the oven of the morning.

In the last sunny dawn, in shorts and sandals, I climb alone to the top of the hill and drink in a thousand mile view, still thirsty for this land/sea/scape. *I can't get enough.*

On the pathway back to the pool, unnamed flowers shimmer like bright candles. I touch their waxy luminous flesh. Linger there. Scarlet bougainvillaea, *fragile paper flames burning in the sun above our coffee & cake.* Will always hang that way. *The way coral breathes forever beneath the ocean, the way tiny yellow crabs scurry endlessly on the beach. The way parrot fish will always brush our legs.* Once I walked alone down one end of the island pulling fine shells up into my skirt. A reef shark nosing the shore. Remembering the pool, the brown splashing bodies of our children, caught forever, suspended in a ray of turquoise light.

Snorkeling In The Coral Reefs

My mermaid daughter floats above the boiling-kettle sand. Translucent sky lifts her into my arms. She is weightless. Ecstatic. Little daughter with the shimmering marlin eyes. Your pupils almost blind me. In them I see a school of beautiful angel fish. Their quick lemons, *fire-opal skin*, tiny mouths and creature eyes. You've snorkeled inside a dream. You fintail around me, my feet hot-stepping in the steaming sand. Telling me about tall tangerine anemones, pink & violet corals, your small girl's hand cupped in your Dad's. Silver and turquoise lateral lines, many dark green tubefish that move like a carpet, *dorsal fins dance against your wrist*. Vivid costumes of clown and parrot fish. My daughter's hands are soft with the sea. She weaves a spell. There's an underwater Eden where shy creatures dart like marzipan fruit. Swim through her sweet hair in waves of salt & sugary colour. She grins, *"I've had the best day of my life!"* Radiates pure joy like a starfish. *It pulls me in.*

The next afternoon, with black mask & snorkel and stiff rubber fins, my nine-year-old daughter with the long, dark-brown hair, my own lovely west coast fish who swam out of my flesh, takes me snorkeling. Takes her mother with her fear of deep water by the hand. We bake in the tropical sun in a long blue skiff with no lifejackets, motoring far out in the milky blue sea. Our island is distant, palms tiny, *farther than I can swim.* This is not the same coral reef as yesterday. My daughter slips into the water and calls me in. I adjust my mask, *wear my brave mother face.* It is dark and deep below. My heart pounds, sharks swim, *a cold cave houses the dead.* We part the ocean, nontropical, *out of our depth,* fins kicking. I wish my Piscean husband were here. He could dispel my fear, swim effortlessly, come up for air, *body and eyes shining with the sea.* We snorkel safely over the abyss towards shallow turquoise water, a coral atoll. My daughter's hair flows like brown kelp, guides me. We gently touch fragile reefs, feel the long low aquarium of water barely covering our backs. I can almost touch the exquisite fish. I breathe easier in the shallow sublime sea. *Bubbles blossom from our masks.*

When it's time to go back, my daughter goes first. Back over the abyss. I follow bravely behind her. By the boat, relaxed bodies of other tourists swim playfully underwater. A fat headless swimmer bobs beneath the surface. Wet with relief, I reach the skiff and haul myself into its crowded hull. Smile triumphantly towards the shore. "Well done Mom," says my Mermaid daughter. Some children are fearless, guiding their parents, *with necessity,* out of their depth.

Tropical Rain

If our roof were made of metal we could hear rain on the West Coast, like they hear rain in Australia, thrumming loud rain.

Where tree frogs with voices as deep as caves bark through the night and we sleep or never sleep. Move our hands *like thunder or clouds*. Bodies full as dams. Mouths open like flowers. Ears cupped to the noisy rhythm of *drummer cicadas*, chirping clicking *long-horned grasshoppers*. Tepid jazzy fingers of powerful rain. Refrain after refrain.

There thunder snaps & Old Spider (large as a small white crab), comes down to make its elastic evening web. The size of a barn door. *Arachne of the roof.* Insects lives stop there. But not the slippery rain.

Then quiet as quiet can be, the sky pulls up her dark skirts. Black velvet over a throat. Quiet as a naked moon. I hear a thin root gulp. The last fat pearled raindrop disappears. The cyclone-proof house slumbers. Screens silence windows. *Jasmine & warm sky careen.*

My Body Longs For The Heat

What my body misses most is the relaxing sleepy heat, where by late-morning I come home *panting* from the giant vacation beach, slip into a square warm house. A tepid shower cools my feverish thermal core. Then into the lounge with an open book, my mind lost in an Australian adventure about a red desert and wild river. Beyond my chair the world steams upward & disappears.

Here you do not lose weight because there is cold beer, cold wine, cold ice cream, and supper is near bedtime and sits around your waist, or rolls to your thighs, wide open on the sweaty bed. The hotness floats through the house; its friendly body calms you, opens you like a *ruby warataw*. Holds you, *says slow down*. Relax. Evaporates worries. Extracts annoying rough grains of stress. Smoothed-out wrinkles. Turns us carefree, languid as lizards. Our lips open slowly, eyes dreamy as we peel a fresh banana, look out at the stars. Our busy bee culture forgotten. Our hive faraway, *another planet*.

With this heat you are always thirsty. I drink tall cylinders of clear water, hold orange paw paw, *like giant butternut squash,* the fresh sweet juice running down my hot throat, *spilling between my sweaty breasts.* The tropical air dries clothes, bright bathing suits in minutes, our skin the colour of roasted almonds. The pungent memory of salt & vinegar, the scented talisman of sunscreen. A crackling newspaper full of shark and chips. How my tongue wants to savour again a chilly bottle of lemonade under the gum trees. And on a bright day listen to cheeky kookaburras laugh recklessly in their kingfisher coats.

When we return to damp Canada, wet *Salt Spring Island,* it's still winter, *end of January.* In the rain we run out of firewood and burn the old grey fence. Brown as tourists we grow verdant moss under our fingernails, dream torrid dreams, *shudder* when sweaters graze our skin. A damp chill permeates our house, pushes its freezing breath, its blue nose under doors. Terrifies us with its foggy face beyond black sheets of glass. Wants to suck our hearth *lifeless,* bury our summer memories with its silver icicle spade.

I fight back and jack up the heat like a bad tenant—to hell with the hydro bill. I throw everything I can burn on the wood fire. Put red salsa, green jalapeño peppers on my food, play Australian music, listen to the haunting didgeridoo. *Imagine a frying sun, our bodies hot as bacon.* Then a refreshing *plunge* in the ocean's balmy bay. By the winter fire we *glisten* in loose shorts and butterfly sulas, lounge naked, suntan lines exposed, white road tracks from two months of tropical travelling. *Defy & defy winter.*

For years my body, my skin holds the hot memory of each penetrating star of heat like a tranquilizer. A *peaceful sunny apéritif* that soothes my ragged nerves, opens me to a necessary lazy & desirous state, *a tropical province.* A burning romance with the sun.

Epilogue

"You loved me as a loser, but now you're worried that I just might win. You know the way to stop me, but you don't have the discipline. How many nights I prayed for this, to let my work begin."

—Leonard Cohen.

Song in the Restless Hours, Waiting For Spring

I am greedy for Time the way the wind lays up against the side of a golden arbutus and shoots straight into the tall blue sailing days. I am greedy for a meal of the measureless sun. The lay-me-down smell of dried grass by the ocean. I'm hungry for the erotic sweetness of fresh figs. I am greedy for life in my tower, for the end of slavery, for the burning of mortgages, for my ship to come in. I am greedy for the wild dancing anarchy crows, for the coal freedom-talk of the raven. The ocean washing over our black boots, eliminating all our tyrannies. Restless with the cubes of hours, *autumn blue, winter bark, polished seeds,* trees bow in the November wind. The last leaf flies off giving me notice. I'm greedy for the winning embrace of my love, and I am triumphant against the dangerous quarrels. I'm greedy for impossible peace. I'm greedy for the writ of Success. I am greedy for the floating gull, its singing fish song, the winter jay, *the naked ice on the naked pond.* The longer minutes I can beg from the winding-down bleak sun. When winter is nothing other than one long wet grey line, one unbroken white zero, *edging, thawing.* I'm greedy for the February greenhouse. The spooning in of seeds.

Hot bouquets of colour caught in tiny distilled planets,
potent, circling, *sexual*. The longings that never fail us.
The seasons, the personal, the destinies. To devour, sweet
vitality. This life. This life. *All this living*